ROUND Is a TORTILLA

A Book of Shapes

By Roseanne Greenfield Thong
Illustrated by John Parra

McGraw Hill Education

Round are *sombreros*.
Round is the moon.
Round are the trumpets
that blare out a tune.

Round are *campanas* that chime and ring.

Round are the nests where swallows sing.

Round are *tortillas* and *tacos*, too.
Round is a pot of *abuela's* stew.
I can name more round things. Can you?

Square are the letters—we know them well.
Square is a board game to help us spell.

Square are *ventanas*
that give a view.
Square is my clock,
and my photos, too.

Square is the park, and the *zócalo*.
Square is a fountain from long ago.
How many square things do you know?

Rectangles are carts
 with bells that chime
and cold *paletas*
 in summertime.

Stone *metates* inside our *casa* help us grind our corn to *masa*.

Rectangles are flags that fly
above the scoreboard, way up high.
How many rectangles do you spy?

Triangles are crunchy chips for *guacamole* and other dips.

Sandías chilled in tubs of ice,
 quesadillas by the slice—
triangles can beat the heat.
 What other triangles can you eat?

Oval is my favorite locket,
   a special pebble in my pocket.

I find ovals at the store,
   huevos, olives, beans galore.
Can you name a couple more?

Stars for parties, stars for light,
 lining streets with colors bright.
 There are so many shapes wherever you go.
 How many more shapes do you know?

GLOSSARY

ABUELA: Grandmother.

ABUELA'S STEW (POZOLE): Grandmothers love to make a special stew called *pozole* on the weekends. *Pozole* is made with *hominy* (large kernels of corn soaked in lime water and dried), and often contains pork, chili, seasonings, and vegetables.

ATÚN: Tuna.

CAMPANAS: Bells. Large *campanas* hang in church towers throughout South and Central America, and chime before celebrations and church services to let worshippers know that it's time to start.

CASA: House.

CUADRADO: Square.

FAMILIA: Family.

GUACAMOLE: A mixture of mashed avocado, chopped onion, tomato, chili pepper, and seasoning, served as a dip for chips or in salads.

HUEVOS: Eggs.

MARIACHIS: Musicians who stroll through the streets (or nowadays play in restaurants), dressed in fine suits with wide-brimmed hats, and who sing ballads accompanied by guitars, trumpets, and violins.

MASA: Corn flour, eaten daily and used for Mexican foods like *tamales* (packets of filled, steamed dough) and *tortillas*.

METATE: A flat or slightly hollowed piece of rock, used with a stone rolling pin called a *mano*. Between the rock and the rolling pin, grain is crushed into meal.

PALETAS: Mexican-style ice-cream or frozen-fruit bars on sticks. Traditional fruit-bar flavors include mango, guava, tamarind and pineapple, and ice-cream flavors include vanilla, chocolate, strawberry, and coconut.

PLAZAS: Public squares or marketplaces.

QUESADILLA: A *tortilla* folded over a filling of hot, melted cheese.

SANDÍA: Watermelon.

SOMBRERO: A Mexican hat made of straw or felt, with a pointed top and an extra-wide brim to shade the head, neck, and shoulders. The name comes from the Spanish word *sombra*, which means "shade."

SUEÑOS: Dreams.

TACO: A *tortilla*, sometimes folded, sometimes flat, piled with fillings like ground meat, cheese, and lettuce, and served hot.

TORTILLAS: Large, round, flatbread pancakes, made from *masa* (corn flour dough) or wheat, and baked on a hot surface. (In Spain, *tortillas* are thick egg omelets fried with potatoes.)

VENTANAS: Windows.

ZÓCALO: Every town and city in Mexico has a *zócalo* or main square, often filled with shady trees, gardens, benches, and fountains. People young and old gather to chat, rest, look at artwork, and listen to bands and entertainers.

mhreadingwonders.com

978-0-07-678750-0
MHID 0-07-678750-8